SHOUT IT OUT
WELL VERSED
REFLECTIONS.
IMAGES AND VERSE

MICHAEL McMANUS

For Elle and Isla
And for you, the reader.
I hope you enjoy my artwork and verses.

CONTENTS

Page

Acknowledgments   v

1   Not all   1

2   Jack from the back   3

3   Animal absurdity   4

4   Dances with the fairies   5

5   The sugar witch   7

6   The nose hair fashionista   9

7   Start of day   11

8   When I lay with the tinker's daughter   13

9   Spellbound   15

10   The crucifix   17

11   My exploitative lover   19

12   Trotters   21

13   Plodging at Seagull City   23

14   Smart is hard, dumb is easy   25

15   A long slow death   27

16   The vane man in the flat cap   29

17   My God   30

18	The robin	31
19	Over ponderous	32
20	Fish and chips and sad jokes	34
21	Gloomy Joe	36
22	Our back fields to Durham	38
23	If everything was right	40
24	The brutal gardener	42
25	Two old girls	44
26	Tommy	45
27	A friendship	46
28	My lost wave	48
29	The man of ritual	50
30	Seat of learning	52
31	The Facebook voyeur	54
32	Hairy eye syndrome	55
33	Dad	56
34	Mam	58
35	Prayer through space junk	60
36	Not my granddaughter	62
37	Sex addiction	63

38   Cursed   65

39   Top knot   67

SHOUT IT OUT

Thanks to Pinterest, from which I took many image
references for the artwork here.

1 NOT ALL

Portrait of The Thinker. Acrylic on canvas

He spoke to me frank, thinker's wisdom unfurls,
As we paint life's complexities, with myriad swirls.
"Not all," is the mantra, as perspective conveys.
A canvas of truth and understanding arrays.

"Not all Pirates sail seas," he sadly did say,
With eyes that saw deeper, in a wise kind of way.
Everyone, a toned shade of grey,
In this unclear world, where perceptions hold sway.

"Not all Cowboys on horses ride," he'd declare,
A reminder that identities aren't always clear.
With acrylic strokes, the canvas they share,
Stories untold and truths to revere.

"Not all labels fit, not all judgments are just,"
He whispered these truths, in a world full of trust.
As the thinker's words painted in colours robust,
A masterpiece of understanding, born to discuss.

With a nod, I concurred, as the truth we'd portray,
Life's canvas is varied in its vibrant display.
In acrylic and canvas, we'll let colours convey,
That diversity thrives in every shade of our day.

2 JACK FROM THE BACK

Jack from the back. Soft Pastel

Brave sailor Jack, upon the shore he stands,
With weathered face and steady loyal hands.
He's seen the world, its wonders and its storms,
Now walks away from ships to other forms.

The sea's his love, its secrets in his eyes,
But now, beneath the boundless open skies
He'll find a different life on solid ground
As waves and wind no longer keep him bound.

With memories of adventures on the sea
He'll find new journeys, new horizons he,
Though ships may fade, the sailor's heart stands
strong,
As Jack walks away, no more his salty song.

3 ANIMAL ABSURDITY

A quick red fox with bright yellow socks
Digital image with Apple Pencil on Ipad.

A flying pig
In a lawyer's wig
Launched high in a car
Aimed straight for a star
And a big brown bear
In pink underwear
With a quick red fox
With bright yellow socks
In a giant shoe
That was hardly new
Went too.

4 DANCES WITH THE FARIES

A girl who danced with the fairies. Watercolour.

In the world of fairies, so enchanting and bright,
Where moonbeams dance and stars take flight,
Do you still reside, in that mystical land,
Where magic and wonder go hand in hand?

Beneath the toadstool's umbrella of green,
In a realm where fantasy is often seen,
Do you frolic with sprites in the shimmering light,
Where dreams come to life every single night?

The fairies, they whisper, and the flowers all sing,
In a place where imagination takes wing,
Do you join their revels, so joyously free,
In the world of the fairies, do you still be?

With wings of gossamer, ethereal grace,
In that wondrous world, do you find your place?
Where wishes take form, and laughter takes flight,
In the realm of the fairies, do you still live tonight?

5 THE SUGAR WITCH

Portrait of The Sugar Witch. Digital image with Apple Pencil on Ipad.

In a hidden kitchen, where secrets reside,
Lived the Sugar Witch, in shadows she'd hide.
Her cauldron, not filled with potions so grim,
But cakes of sweetness, her wickedest whim.

Tobacco was sugar in her mystic spell,
She'd bake it in cakes, a mysterious smell.
A world turned sweet, her creations would cast,
A sugary spell, a sweetness so vast.

Each cake she conjured, a sugary dream,
Tobacco turned sugar, or so it would seem.
Her magic transformed the bitter and dry,
Into desserts that made taste buds flicker and fly.

Take caution my friend, of the sugar's embrace,
Indulgence in excess is a perilous chase.
The Sugar Witch's magic, a tempting display,
But in her world of sweetness, you might lose your
way.

Beware oh beware Sugar Witch's delight,
For too much of sweetness can cloud our foresight.
In her cakes of wonder, there's a lesson to learn,
That balance in life is the sweetest return.

6 THE NOSE-HAIR FASHIONISTA

Portrait of The Nose-hair Fashionista.

In the mirror I spy a sight, long nose-hairs, dear, oh my!
They dance and sway with every breath as I let out a sigh,
For some they're signs of aging's grace, a badge of years gone by,
But I can't help but wish they'd trim and not let them reach the sky.

Though age is just a number, they say, it's hard to not feel shy,
Long nose-hairs whisper tales of time, as they reach down, far too high,
And as they gather dust and muck, I can't help but wonder why
They don't snip them, clip them, groom them, so

their nose-hair can say goodbye.

But let's remember, it's just a phase, a challenge to
defy,
Long nose-hairs may make us frown, but there's no
need to moan and cry.
A little trim, a touch of care, and we'll be flying high,
No more feeling like we're aged, just fashion,
youthful, spry.

In that hot world of fashion, where trends take flight
each day,
Nose-hair becomes my accessory, oh so bright and
gay!
Styled and trimmed, one nostril - a unique sight to
bear,
Fashion nose-hair on the town, my statement brave
and rare.

7 START OF DAY

Portrait of a man who starts his day with porridge and a hymn. Graphite.

Do you still start your day with a bowl of porridge
and a hymn?
In a world so fast paced, where the rush never seems
to dim,
There's a comfort in traditions, a melody of the past,
As morning light filters through, casting memories
that last.

A bowl of steaming porridge, warm and hearty
embrace,
Nourishing body and soul, a simple breakfast's grace,
And a hymn, a song of solace, to start the day anew,
With words that touch the spirit, like morning's gentle
dew.

In this modern age of chaos, where time forever flies,
Let us not forget these moments, beneath the open
skies,
For in the quiet rituals, a connection we may find,
To the essence of our being, to the peace of heart and
mind.

So, do you still start your day with a bowl of porridge
and a hymn?
In a world that's ever-changing, where the future's
light is dim,
Take a pause, embrace the stillness, let these
traditions guide,
And find the inner harmony where the soul and heart
collide.

8 WHEN I LAY WITH THE TINKER'S DAUGHTER

Portrait of the Tinker's Daughter's horse.
Watercolour

When I lay with the Tinker's daughter, under the stars
so bright,
Beneath the vast celestial canvas, on a magical
moonlit night.
Her eyes, like constellations held secrets yet untold,
In a timeless frenzied moment, our true love story
told.

We whispered dreams and wishes to the cool night's
soft embrace,
As the gentle breeze kissed our cheeks and time
slowed down its pace.
With every stolen kiss our hearts beat in sweet refrain,
Under the canopy of stars, bodily harmony wild,
insane.

The Tinker's daughter and I, two souls forever

entwined,
In the tapestry of the cosmos, our love forever
defined.
Underneath the starry heavens, our destinies aligned,
A story written in stardust; a love memory forever
enshrined.

Awakening at sunrise, by the Tinker's daughter's side,
Her gentle presence soothes, in the morning's golden
tide.
Her horse, a silent companion, grazes with grace
untamed,
In this tranquil moment, love's beauty was
proclaimed.

9 SPELLBOUND

Portrait of the man of spells. Watercolour

In a hidden corner of the mystic town,
There dwells a man of spells, of great renown,
He sells his wares, a curious display,
A master of the craft in every way.

With incantations whispered soft and low,
He weaves enchantments in a secret glow,
From potions brewed in ancient cauldrons deep,
To whispered curses in the night's dark sweep.

He cures warts with herbs, a gentle touch,
Turning warts to dust with spells and such,
Yet, in the shadows, his true art unfurls,
With voodoo dolls and magic's deepest swirls.

He tells fortunes with cards and crystal clear,

Peering into destinies both far and near,
Unravelling the tapestry of time's embrace,
Revealing futures in his sacred space.

But in the heart of his arcane artistry,
Lies the voodoo doll's profound mystery,
With pins and stitches, he weaves his spell,
In the name of magic, where stories dwell.

He binds intentions with threads of fate,
In the voodoo doll's small, potent state,
For his power, a bridge to realms unknown,
A tapestry of secrets carefully sewn.

A man of many talents, in shadows veiled,
Where realms of wonder and mystery are hailed,
He sells not just spells, but a world apart,
A journey through magic, for every heart.

10 THE CRUCIFIX

A Birthday Gift in 1953 (from my Teacher, Sister
Mary Agnes)

In cloistered halls where wisdom's light does gleam,
A nun bestowed a gift, a sacred dream,
A crucifix of wood, a symbol pure,
To bless and guide, its meaning to endure.

With tender words, she bid me go,
To priest's abode, where blessings freely flow,
I took the cross, entrusted in my care,
To seek the priest's solemn blessing there.

Returned, the crucifix, now blessed anew,
I placed it in the nun's kind hands, her due.
Yet on my birthday's dawn, a joy untold,
The nun returned the cross, a gift to hold.

A surprise so sweet, a gesture so sincere,
She wished me joy on this my special year,
The crucifix, a token of her love,
A symbol shared from heaven above.

In humble grace, our spirits intertwined,
A bond of faith, our lives forever bind,
The boy, the teacher-nun, the crucifix, a sign,
Of blessings passed, a connection so divine.

And now, fully embracing doubt,
My soul takes flight to Atheism's rout.
Yet in a corner of my heart's abode
A flicker of faith in a different code – the act of
human kindness.

11 MY EXPLOITATIVE LOVER

Portrait of my exploitative lover. Digital image with
Apple Pencil on Ipad.

In shadows she appeared, a captivating prize,
With a tender smile that hid her cunning eyes.
A woman of allure, a master of disguise,
Using my kindness, in her web of lies.

I opened my heart, my trust laid bare,
Unaware of the traps, the hidden snare.
She danced through my world with deceptive grace,
Manipulating my vulnerability to her wicked embrace.

Her words like honey, sweet and beguiling,
Yet beneath the surface, deceit was compiling.
Exploiting my warmth, my caring open heart,
Tearing my world and trust apart.

But through this trial, I've learned to stand strong,
To recognize deceit, to admit when I'm wrong.
For in darkness, we find the strength to arise,
And heal the wounds from such unkind lies.

12 TROTTERS

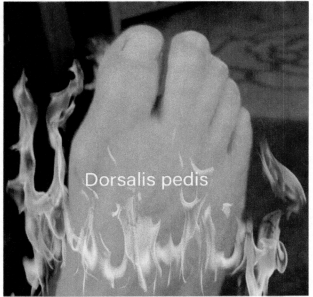

Trotters, (my feet).

In a world where feet found no equals,
Lived a man with peculiar pedestals,
Some said that his 'cloven hooves,' they'd declare,
'Dorsalis pedis' like the devil's, a sinister affair.

His behaviour, they claimed, matched the dark view,
As if a demon's shadow in the morning dew,
Yet I found them strangely calming, in truth,
Would gaze upon those feet from my youth.

A mystery wrapped in a curious guise,
These trotters of his, under cloudy skies,
For while some feared the devil's grin,
I sensed a quiet peace, hidden within.

His feet, like pigs' trotters, unique and rare,

An enigma that stirred the whispers in the air,
And though judgments raged like a tempestuous sea,
I saw a different story in those feet, wild and free.

For what may seem strange or sinister at first glance,
Could hold a deeper truth, a hidden romance,
In the footsteps of a man with feet untamed,
I found a lesson in acceptance, not to be blamed.

13 PLODGING AT SEAGULL CITY

Plodging at Seagull City. Watercolour.

In Seagull City, where my roots did sprout,
I found a haven, a place to sing and shout.
Sunderland's embrace, my genesis and more,
A love for this coastal town I deeply adore.

Seagulls danced on waves, their cries in the breeze,
As I wandered the shore, plodging at ease.
The sea, an eternal canvas, shifting and wide,
In its soothing rhythm, I found solace inside.

From Roker Pier to the Wearmouth Bridge's grace,
Every corner held a special, cherished place.
A symphony of memories, laughter, and fun,
In Sunderland, my journey had just begun.

In Seagull City, my heart found its way,

A love that forever in my soul will stay.
My genesis, my roots, in this city of brine,
The Barbary Coast and The East End sublime.

14 SMART IS HARD, DUMB IS EASY

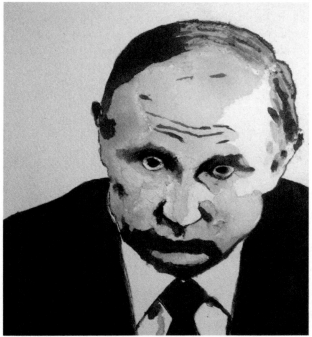

Portrait of Vladimir Putin. Watercolour.

I don't want to sound arrogant, I truly believe,
In humility's grace, I aim to achieve,
But let me share a thought, if I may,
In hopes it sheds some light on our day.

In a world where knowledge's torch does burn,
You can present some smart idea, to discern,
A comment, truth, a beacon of the wise,
Yet most people follow the less smart, to my surprise.

Because smart is hard and dumb is easy,
The masses are asses, it seems so seedy,
They opt for simplicity over the learned view,

In this curious paradox, their choices ensue.

Look at Trump and Johnson and Putin, examples of
this tale,
Where celebrity and silly talk prevails over facts, truth,
and detail,
In the theatre of politics, a reflection we find,
Of a world where wisdom and truth can be left far
behind.

15 A LONG SLOW DEATH

Portrait of a woman whose 'gaze, a dagger, pierced my soul'. Oil on canvas.

Knowing you has been like a long slow death,
A bittersweet journey, every fleeting breath.
In your presence, I've withered, day by day,
But your memory lingers, it won't fade away.

Like autumn leaves, our moments fell,
Each one a story, too fragile to tell.
Your gaze, a dagger, pierced my soul,
Yet in your absence, I'm not whole.

Through the darkness, we both strayed,
Lost in the promises we never made.
In the end, it's clear to see,
Knowing you was my destiny.

SHOUT IT OUT

Though it hurt, I won't regret,
The love we shared, the suns that set.
For even in this slow demise,
I found a beauty in your eyes.

16 THE VANE MAN IN THE FLAT CAP

Portrait of The Vane Man in the Flat Cap

In the crowded street, he strolls along,
The man in the flat cap, so worldly and strong,
With a twinkle in his eye and a confident stride,
He carries a charm that's hard to hide.

In his cap, stories of years gone by,
Echoes of laughter and tears he can't deny,
A lifetime of memories etched in that cap,
The man in the flat cap, a walking map.

He greets each day with a knowing smile,
Life's twists and turns, he's known for a while,
In the rhythm of the city he's found his place,
The man in the flat cap, a timeless grace.

17 MY GOD

Portrait of God; angry at the state of the world but doing nothing whatsoever about it. Soft pastel.

The power over life and death
Is said, solely in God's realm.
By The Lord we live and Lord we die.
God gives and takes from you and I.

My God though is the Surgeon,
Who's saved me from demise.
Powered over my life
And brought me back to rise.

18 THE ROBIN

The Robin. Watercolour.

Amidst the Autumn's fading song,
A robin perches, looking strong.
As Winter's chill begins to near,
We watch her from our warm frontier.

With feathers ruffled, brave and bold,
She bears the pain, heroism's ode.
In snow-kissed trees, she finds her way,
A symbol of hope on a Wintry day.

19 OVER PONDEROUS

Portrait of a woman I know who is over-ponderous.
Digital image with Apple Pencil on iPad.

In the fathoms of thoughts, you roam so deep,
Where contemplation's secrets you do keep.
But, my dear friend, I gently say to thee,
Sometimes, you're over-ponderous, don't you see?

Your mind, a labyrinth of intricate schemes,
Navigating complexities, chasing dreams.
Yet, during your profound embrace,
Remember, not all answers dwell in that space.

Life's rhythm dances, a delicate waltz,
Sometimes, simplicity has more exalts.
You're over-ponderous, my dear, it's true,
Let moments flow, let spontaneity ensue.

SHOUT IT OUT

In the stillness of silence, there's a song,
A melody of life, where you belong.
So, cherish the balance, don't over-weigh,
For in the lightness of being, you'll find your way.

20 FISH AND CHIPS AND SAD JOKES

Portrait of a man who publishes sad jokes and pics of
fish and chips on Facebook. Watercolour.

On Facebook's stage, a man does play,
With sad jokes and food on display.
His humour, though, may lack finesse,
Yet let's not judge, but rather bless.

For in this world of diverse streams,
Not all inspire intellectual dreams.
His harmless simplicity has its place,
Adding a smile to our digital space.

Amidst the complex and profound,
A simple joy in what he's found.
Fish and chips, a humble grace,
In their own way, they too embrace.

SHOUT IT OUT

In a world of culture, wide and vast,
Each voice, a note in the grand contrast.
Let's cherish the man with his unique style,
For on Facebook's canvas, he too adds a smile.

21 GLOOMY JOE

Portrait of Gloomy Joe. Watercolour.

In the corner of a dim-lit café, there's Joe,
His demeanour as grey as the clouds that hang low.
With eyes like shadows, and a heart heavy with woe,
He's known in this town as Gloomy Joe.

He sips his black coffee, his thoughts far away,
Lost in a world where the skies are always grey.
His face rarely brightens, his laughter's in tow,
For life's burdens have made him Gloomy Joe.

But if you sit with him and lend an ear,
You'll find in his stories, there's much to endear.
For beneath his façade, a wisdom does flow,
A depth of emotion in Gloomy Joe.

He's weathered life's storms, seen its highs and its
lows,
Felt the weight of its sorrows, endured its hard blows.
Yet, still, he persists, in the face of the foe,
There's strength in the spirit of Gloomy Joe.

So, don't judge him harshly, this man of the shade,
For within his soul, a resilience is laid.
In his world of darkness, there's a flicker, a glow,
A quiet kind of beauty in Gloomy Joe.

22 OUR BACK FIELDS TO DURHAM

Back-fields to Durham. From Hopper's Wood.
Watercolour.

In Durham's heart, where history blends with grace,
Lies a landscape, a tranquil, timeless space.
Our backfields stretch, a patchwork quilt of green,
A countryside tapestry, a living dream.

The River Wear meanders, crystal clear,
Its gentle flow, a whispered song to hear.
As rolling hills embrace this ancient scene,
In Durham's backfields, nature reigns as queen.

The sun, a golden brush, paints fields aglow,
With hues of amber, crimson, soft indigo.
In every season, beauty here resides,
In changing landscapes, nature's art abides.

Beneath the vast expanse of open skies,
Where larks and swallows gracefully arise,
Wildflowers bloom, a rainbow on the earth,
A testament to nature's boundless worth.

Oh, Durham City, with your backfields grand,
A sanctuary where the soul can stand,
And in the quiet, find a peaceful grace,
A timeless beauty, nature's warm embrace.

23 IF EVERYTHING WAS RIGHT

Portrait of Elle and Isla's 'uphill climb....dawn
emerges from darkest night'.. Graphite.

In life's tapestry of twists and turns,
A paradox in each lesson learned:
If all was right, no shadows cast,
Would we truly cherish moments past?

For sweetness blooms in contrast's embrace,
In shadows' dance and challenges we face,
If skies were always clear and bright,
Would stars still dazzle in endless night?

The bitter taste, the uphill climb,
They lend the heart its rhythm, its rhyme,
If everything flowed as a tranquil stream,
Would spirits yearn, would we dare to dream?

SHOUT IT OUT

The jagged edges, the stormy skies,
They sculpt our strength, make us realise,
That diamonds form 'neath pressure's might,
And dawn emerges from darkest night.

So let storms rage and trials persist,
In life's ebb and flow, we truly exist,
For if everything was flawless and pure,
Appreciation's flame might not endure.

24 THE BRUTAL GARDENER

Portrait of the Brutal Gardener. Oil on canvas.

In a garden once lush, with colours so bright,
Stalked a brutal woman, a fearsome blight.
With a heart that was cold, and hands just like steel,
She tore through the blooms, with unending zeal.

Lovely flowers trembled, petals in fear,
As she approached, their doom drawing near.
Her fingers like daggers, ruthless and keen,
Ripped out the blossoms, in a heartless routine.

Where roses once flourished, now silence remained,
Her devastation, a garden's loss gained.
The fragrance of life now replaced by despair,
A paradise ruined, beyond all repair.

Yet even in darkness, a glimmer of hope,

As nature's resilience begins to elope.
New sprouts will arise, through sorrow and strife,
To mend what was shattered, to breathe in new life.

For gardens may falter, but they never truly die,
They rise from the ashes, under the same sky.
Brutal reign shall subside, flowers become vast,
And the garden shall bloom, reclaiming its past.

25 TWO OLD GIRLS

Two Old Girls. Digital image with Apple Pencil on
Ipad.

Two old ladies, hand in hand,
Along the coastal path they stand.
With weathered faces, eyes so bright,
They walk together, side by side.

The salty breeze, the crashing waves,
Their friendship strong, like ocean's embrace.
Stories shared and laughter's sound,
As they journey along the sandy ground.

Memories woven with each step they take,
A bond unbreakable, no distance can shake.
The coastal path, their chosen guide,
Two old girls walking, side by side.

26 TOMMY

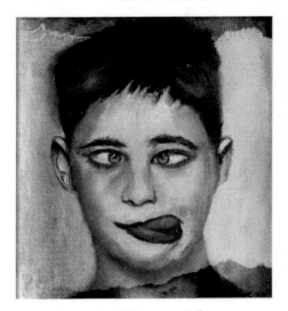

Portrait of Tommy. Oil on canvas.

Tommy the spoiler, oh what a trickster,
In every photograph, he's quite the fixer.
A sly grin and mischief in his eyes,
He adds a twist, catching us by surprise

Snapshots of moments, memories so dear,
Tommy sneaks in, his intentions clear.
A funny hat or a quirky pose,
He turns every picture into a joyful pose.

27 A FRIENDSHIP

A Friendship. Taken when the pair visited my garden
one evening.

In moonlit glades, where secrets gleam,
A hedgehog and a cat did dream.
With quills so sharp and fur so sleek,
They met by night, no words to speak.

The hedgehog's spines, a fortress strong,
A shield against the world's cruel throng.
Yet in its heart, a longing grew,
For friendship's touch and skies so blue.

The cat, a dancer in the dark,
Moved with grace, left nary a mark.
Its eyes aglow, like stars above,
It sought companionship and love.

They danced beneath the silver light,
A duo born of whimsy's flight.
Two souls so different, yet the same,
Bound by fate's enchanting game.

Through shadows deep and moonlit trails,
They forged a bond that never pales.
With hedgehog's caution and cat's flair,
Together, they were quite a pair.

So if you find yourself one night,
Beneath the stars' soft, glowing light,
Remember well this tale so true,
Of hedgehog and cat, and friendship's hue.

28 MY LOST WAVE

Portrait of a man who waved at a woman on
Facebook. Watercolour.

I waved to a woman on Facebook's shore,
With a virtual gesture, a smile I wore,
But in the sea of posts, she sailed on by,
Leaving my wave lost, a digital sigh.

In the world of likes, shares, and friends,
I hoped for a connection, a message that sends,
But her gaze passed over, a fleeting glance,
Leaving my gesture in a lonely dance.

In the pixels and screens, we sail our ships,
In a vast online world, where connection slips,
A wave, the simple act of reaching out,
Can sometimes get lost in the digital rout.

But I'll keep on waving in the cyber sea,
For a chance encounter, a moment to be,
Perhaps one day our paths will align,
And in that moment, our friendship will shine.

29 THE MAN OF RITUAL

Portrait of The Man of Ritual. Watercolour.

Morning appears, his scripted scenes begin, rigid,
A symphony of habits, a rehearsed overture,
regimented,
Coffee poured, the ritual's first act,
The day's curtain rises on familiar gestures,
He revels in the predictability, the comfort he craves.

Like, a mystic man of the past, anointing with
aromatic oils,
Symbols traced on his weathered skin,
Chanting echoes through the void,
A dance of mystic, timeless kin, now gone,
Over and over and over again, he repeats the
mundane.

And there he goes again, a carbon copy,

No spontaneity in his well-trod path,
On life's stage, he enacts his scenes.
In the cadence of habit, he finds solace,
A scripted existence, his chosen opus.

Like a Druid's silent steps on sacred ground,
Volcanic glass, an obsidian cloak, a shroud of secrets.
In repetition, comfort blooms, security, the known,
He dances through the mundane haze,
The Man of Ritual, a stoic performer.

End of day, candles flicker, dance with whispers,
Incantations weave the unseen,
Glyph-like tapestry of the night,
His communion with realms unknown, until
tomorrow,
A choreography of endless days, and nights, the same.

30 SEAT OF LEARNING

View from the Seat of Learning

Seat in a passion-space
A sheltered place,
Hormones apace
A frenzied spot,
Leafed branches, thick
To hide the plot.
To love and learn, and then,
Return to love and learn again
And again.

Seat beside the river sweet,
A special place
That was our own
We talked and touched
And kissed and clutched
Gasping much in fevered charge.

Such joy those times; heavenly sublimes
Now set deep in memory,
Frequently refreshed.

31 THE FACEBOOK VOYEUR

Portrait of The Facebook Voyeur. Graphite.

He lingers on Facebook's digital street,
A voyeur, silent, in his quiet seat,
No posts to share, no words to convey,
He watches from shadows, night and day.

Invisible, he scrolls through each friend's life,
A silent spectator, free from strife,
He learns their stories, their joys, and despair,
A Facebook voyeur, no content to share.

32 HAIRY EYE SYNDROME

Hairy Eye Syndrome

In the thoughts of whimsy and the absurd,
There's a tale of a syndrome, quite unheard.
It's called "hairy eye," a curious delight,
Where sight meets fuzz in the softest light.

Eyes adorned with a furry surprise,
Lashes like moss 'neath enchanted skies.
In the night of dreams, where oddities gleam,
Hairy eye syndrome, a whimsical theme.

But remember, my friend, it's just in jest,
In the world of reality, put it to rest.
For eyes so adorned with a charming grace,
In their own unique way, find their place.

33 DAD

Dad

A certain loving gaze,
His promise of affection,
Invitation to his knee - accepted.
Red, sensitive, massive hand,
A comb of fingers again and again
Through my boyish hair.

Strong, yet delicate touch,
Comfort, warming, hypnotic friction but
More powerfully
More profoundly
Affection and love:
More than I could ever hope to give.

Conditions of adultness exchanged comb for
handshake
But still as warm.

Now a hug before leaving
So many times.
After the first, and my return, he was sadly moved to
tell me:
"You know Michael, you never looked back at me
and your mam".

But how could I have broken my heart more?
How could I turn
As he would have surely done if me?
How could I know the measure of love that moved a
head like his?

And then his final leaving -
My hopeless expectation of eternal forlornness.
Yet still my attempt to comfort - cureless, combing
hand
Repeatedly on tortured brow, hoping to ease his pain
- and mine.
Now I imagine it helped him leave easier
My pain of conscience eased at least.
Like I could not, I know he must look back
For I still feel his hypnotic love combing, combing,
combing.

34 MAM

Mam

I couldn't bear you not being there
And followed everywhere you went
And only when I closed my eyes
Were you quite ever out of sight.

The day you left me at that school
I thought the end had really come,
It was the start of something new
I was not certain I would like.

I took your net with me to school,
And in the lonely moments there,
I took the drug from secret place
And sniffed your hair - so comforting.

Your sensitive depth of thought,
Too deep at times perhaps for best,

In me I recognise it too,
And learned its use to good avail,

The disappointing days ill spent
Awaiting the return of love
When love did not just quite return,
I saw your face and broke my heart.

I dread the thought how it must be
For one so young without your love?
Without that strong dependency
You gave so constantly to me.

But as with many things alike, now gone,
True value only now is known
Of how it shapes the way you go.
Your influence continues on.

35 PRAYER THROUGH SPACE JUNK

View of Space Junk

Onward to heaven, where prayers are sent,
Beneath the stars, where hopes are dreamt,
A cosmic dance, a cluttered sky,
The prayers ascend, but some deny.

Space junk we've sown, a celestial sea,
It orbits high, where dreams should be,
Prayers deflect in debris' maze,
Yet faith persists through planetary haze.

Though space may deflect their earthly plea,
In hearts, their hopes and prayers break free,
For in the vastness of this stellar tide,
Their dreams endure, on faith some ride.

In the cosmos, their prayers take flight,
But space junk is a celestial blight,
Eighty percent get lost to the scrap,

A cosmic tale, a holy trap.

Among the stars, they send their plea,
Yet debris fills the void, you see,
In heavens vast, their words may wane,
But in some faith endures, through joy and pain.

As space junk scatters hope like rain,
In hearts, all prayers still seek domain,
And faith's a beacon, burning bright, in some,
It guides them through the metal slum.

36 NOT MY GRANDDAUGHTER

Portrait of a girl who was not my granddaughter.
Acrylic on canvas

'Just who on earth do you think you are?' I ask,
You're implying authority, a daunting task.
'You can't tell me what to do,' I state,
Our relationship's clear, no room for debate.

You're not my granddaughter, the evidential truth,
But I hear your command, your words uncouth,
So, take these lines, earnest and true,
A solemn response, from me to you.

'Just who do you think you are?' I plead,
With fervour, I claim, with fiery speed.
'You can't tell me what to do,' I fear,
You're not my granddaughter, so get out of here.

37 SEX ADDICTION

Portrait of temptation, a haunting, relentless ghost.
Watercolour.

In the shadowed halls of a Catholic past,
Where lessons of virtue were meant to last,
A seed was sown, a secret thrived,
A silent struggle within, contrived.
Sex, a haunting, relentless ghost,
Whispering desires, impossible to host.

A convent's walls, a confessional booth,
Battlegrounds for a soul, seeking truth.
Through the tangled maze of desire,
A journey lit by an inner fire.
A doctor, wise, with compassionate eyes,
Guided steps through passion's disguise.

In the therapist's haven, a portrait stands,
A symbol of healing, crafted hands.
A canvas capturing a journey's strife,
A metamorphosis, reclaiming life.
Clean now, in the moment's grace,
A testament to resilience, a triumph to embrace.

The weight of the past, a burden shed,
As time unfolds, the spirit is led.
Aging, a healer, time's gentle touch,
Softening the edges that once were much.
From the shackles of addiction set free,
A phoenix rising, in serenity.

38 CURSED

Portrait of the gypsy girl who cursed me at the horse fair. Acrylic on canvas

In the swirl of Appleby Fair's lively crowd,
I, a whisperer of horses, humbly bowed.
Amidst the vibrant hues of gypsy attire,
Encountered a woman, wrapped in mystic fire.

Her eyes, a universe of secrets untold,
A tale of passion, a story to unfold.
In the dance of horses, whispers exchanged,
A fleeting connection, emotions estranged.

But when desire sought to intertwine,
I declined, leaving sparks to malign.
Her fury ignited, a tempest brewed,

A curse unleashed, dark and shrewd.

Seven days of impotence, a bitter toll,
A saga of shadows, a heartache's scroll.
Horse whispers silenced, passion suppressed,
A week of anguish, a soul distressed.

Yet, in the depths of that cursed despair,
A resilience awakened; a spirit aware.
For curses may linger, but not define,
The essence of a soul, a spirit to realign.

Appleby's fair, a memory cast,
Of horses and curses, moments amassed.
In the echo of hooves and curses unfurl,
A whisperer's tale, a dance with the whirl

39 TOP KNOT

Old Top Knot

In Durham City, an old chap did reside,
His top knot perched high, impossible to hide.
With hair so thin, it seemed almost a prank,
But he flaunted that knot, like a captain his plank.

As folks passed him by, they couldn't help but stare,
At the audacious style of his thinning hair.
Whispers and giggles followed him around,
Yet he grinned right back, with a mischievous sound.

When the wind picked up, oh what a sight to behold,
His knot swayed and wobbled, like a story untold.
But he held his ground, unshaken and stout,
Saying, "Life's too short to worry about hair falling out!"

ABOUT THE AUTHOR

Michael McManus was born in Durham City, UK in 1946. He is a Retired Airman, Royal Navy (1964-1971); Retired Police Officer, Durham Constabulary (1971-1999); Retired Part-time Teacher, University of Durham (1999-2015). He is married to Annette, for 55 years and they live in Durham City. He was awarded a BA (Hons) from the University of Northumbria and a PhD from the University of Durham. He is now a Leisure Painter, Leisure Writer and Leisure Poet.

2023

Printed in Great Britain
by Amazon